The Heart Uncut

Marian Kilcoyne

WORDSONTHESTREET

First published 2020 by

Wordsonthestreet

Six San Antonio Park, Salthill, Galway, Ireland
www.wordsonthestreet.com
publisher@wordsonthestreet.com

ISBN 978-1-907017-55-1

Cover design, layout and typesetting: Wordsonthestreet

For Jake & Lily

Acknowledgements

The author would like to acknowledge the following literary journals where some of these poems, or earlier versions, were first published: *Prelude* (US), *The Louisville Review* (US), *Poetry Salzburg Review* (Austria), *Crannóg* (IRL), *Ofi Press* (Mexico), *The Frogmore Papers* (UK), *Cyphers* (IRL), *Apalachee Review* (US), *Foliate Oak Literary Magazine* (US), *New Contrast* (Cape Town), *Quiddity* (US), *Right Hand Pointing* (US), *Grey Sparrow Journal* (US), *Off The Coast* (US), *The Galway Review* (IRL), *The Liner* (US), *Into The Void* (IRL), *Roanoke Literary Journal* (US), *The Rockhurst Review* (US), *Banshee Literature* (IRL), *The Catamaran Literary Reader* (US), *The Worcester Review* (US), *The Stonecoast Review* (US), *The Main St Rag* (US), *Brushfire Literature & Arts Journal* (US), *Poetry in The Park* (Athlone), *The Poetry collective* (Clare Champion), *The Fredericksburg Literary and Art Review* (US Spring, Summer & Fall 2018), *The Cape Rock: Poetry* (US), *The Curlew* (UK), *Crossways* February 2019, *The Qutub Minar Review* (INTL 2019), *Southbank Poetry* (London 2019).

About the Author

Marian Kilcoyne is an Irish writer based on the west coast of Ireland. She has been a teacher at senior level, worked professionally in education and management for an Aids organization, and reviewed fiction and non-fiction for the *Sunday Business Post*.

She attended the Seamus Heaney Centre's Poetry Summer School at Queen's University Belfast in 2013. She was featured poet on *Poethead – Contemporary Irish women poets*, January 9th – 16th 2018. She was short-listed for the 2017 Dermot Healy International Poetry Award. She was placed on the long-list for the 2019 Fish Poetry Prize. www.mariankilcoyne.com.

Contents

Spectre

When I saw you, the earth went silent.
The chattering birds sawed off their beaks.
The breeze hushed and gulped into itself.
If there was a cicada, it choked on a stone.
The trees donned black tie and straightened
while the mouse, mole and hedgehog died
in their sleep. The fox darted further
into the amaranthine garden, nose quivering,
inhaling fright. When I saw you, the moon
strangled the sun, spat upon the stars.
Now see what you have done.

Collateral Damage

August – bitter morning coffee
slops over wrist, legs and toes,
at the ballistic whack of
a bird on glass.

Pain elapsed, I tiger to where it lies on
cool stone. There I am beaten by my year-old
pup whose mouth is soft for pheasant.
She holds the thrush smoothly,
eyes me slyly while I hush staccato
breaths. We both know the score.

Straining every muscle, I pounce,
forcing her jaw in a flick knife
second. Warm bird, neck broken,
pillows to the ground.

Speckled feathers, sweet head,
were no match for sheet glass illusion,
the marvel of avian construct sabotaged
by its own strange delicacy.

Antibes Reverie

Juked up on citron pressé, gambolling
through the food market in the Cours Massena
I think of you, old man, fine writer, cranky and
built for the fight, fiery individualist. For all that, in your
once chosen home I salute you, but for *J'Accuse** I bow low
to the druid who guided your pen – though your death outpaced
justice. Considering the nature of nerve and guts I buy sturdy
early cherries blanching at the cost, yet dazed as a fool by
their sweet flesh and lip sting stain. The Côte d'Azur sparkles
and shimmies towards a perfumed, sex laden, hot afternoon haze,
along the way, wringing the mist from my west of Ireland bones.
I curl on a stone wall to view the slash design yachts, beauties all,
hiccupping in Port Vauban. Courage is courage, here or there.

*J'Accuse: The Dark Side of Nice by Graham Greene

Because I Like the Interstices More ....

What will survive of us is love
Philip Larkin

There ought not be
someone in the garden
supine earthy and female
but there was
ought not be a time
to be reborn running with
the steely grey sea
there is
There ought not be a time
when religion shut your
mouth woman
there
Ought not be a time
we gazed indolently
at crimes retching inwards
Yes
ought not be a time
we are afraid to be alone
grazing at the altars of politics, god,
and who will mind us now
well
ought not be a time
when we long for the

cradling lap of the leader who
regiments our wayward minds
to one upward convulsion
finding soul
we bend
ought not be a time you
look at her, your eyes blazing so
she sees the pain
knowledge
ought not be a time
men are razed
sundered from maleness
you know
ought not be a time
brain becomes deity
yet yet
ought not be a time
you look at him hungry for
insight or pain
so now
ought not be a man
who got it so right
he may have been wrong.

Girl

Since I saw the girl who does not eat,
or trade in food currency, to keep the
breath even, or the gaze straight. Since
then. Since then ago to now, I cannot
bear to watch a robin hopping nervously
on skinny legs, or jaunting round the
patio, perilously balanced.
Thinking of the Girl, I remember that
no part of her was right. I wondered
if when she crossed her clanking legs, she felt
her skeletal reality, but there was no room in
her for thoughts. None. Her spider web being
flushed all joy from me that day. How heavy her
head must be, I thought.

Sionnach Rua*

This brittle November night drawn taut
with winter concussion, I scope the garden
fretful for events. Brain cradling sepals fall
low, as two eyes, hard shiny and sloe diamond
pin me to the actual, the now.
I grab your eyes – you seize mine, and sidle
into my kitchen sniffing my fare, perusing
my open notebook, marvelling at my pretensions,
watching my sleeping children. You pad on soufflé
paws, the genetic imperative of fear and slouch
rising in the blood and then I know that you visit often,
friend in the dark. Oh, but you are my one recurring
vision and I thought this habitat was mine alone.
The carelessness of the bipedal hominid slack
with casual hubris.

*Red Fox

The Messenger

A *saighneán** wind coursed
through the garden at the
back of my brother's house
on a day so ordinary even
Spite laid down its fingers.
Warning or warming? No, this
entity was benign or fond,
though there was something
in the shimmy of hedge and
scruff that had me set down
my cup roughly and stand
pugilistic, trembling,
clear eyed. The edges of my
mind pleating.
Something was coming, slow,
patient, and ravening.

*saighneán– Lightning flash or streak in the Irish language.
Pronounced Shiv-nawn

Justify Me

For you to feel better I
must feel worse. Shimmying
clandestinely amongst the
shadows of the former
versions of ourselves.
We have shed so many
skins, crumpled jerseys
thrown on the floor.
The shadows I move
between are amoebic blobs
jostling for my attention, craving
to go back to the way it was
before the fall.
For me to feel better, I slam the
door on their creeping hysteria.

Mislaid Days

She feels the tide recede in the mudflats
of her mind as she stones black cherries.
Nothing here but the cherubs, juice,
stained hands roofed to the wrists. Pebbles.
Her mind idles on the spray of purple black,
spreading wildly. Everywhere.
Thoughts try to beach from the mud, tugging
upward, trying for the thing. Life.
Pulled back down, sucked into the brackish mass
fighting to the end. It was a memory, never a
thought and is lost. Bites.
It is what you missed, back then, in your blunder
toward beauty. Courage.

Briar Notes

Faster than light or sound
the night star slinked, arced
and shot to a spot in the
clayground, festooned with
spiky plants.
When my time comes, I want
to slink, arc and shoot to bog
and botanist paradise. My only
witness, the white line of the
shore and the visitor fox holding
his breath.

Liebeslied*

Marsh brown fields clutch bog cotton
in fairy clusters, while the heron lands.
Its harsh 'kaark' a battle cry, shaving
peace from a hazy afternoon. In a moment, you
are born over and over again to this Atlantic
refuge with its teeming silver hues; safe place & padlock.
Close the eyes now to sounds of breaking waves
on the shore. The smell of it, the teasing umami taste
of it on lips forming words. The commotion.

*Love song.

Caveat

Two long winters
waxed and waned
though every time
she tried to spike
them, she failed.

Failed to rise above
the petulant hurt
borne of the snagged
heart. The catch of
the zip of life.

Failed to rid the comet
of its tail of stardust.
The hubris of its plumage.

Failed to see, really see,
the efforts of healing
nestling in. The yolk of
life, blaze of orange.

The Paradox of You

Your face reveals to me layer
after layer. Opening slowly, as
always, an atlas. Page on page,
a country – strange harbour.
Why is it that you take years
to do this uncoiling?

Even excavators have their
limits, throwing in the trowel,
kicking the dust into the cosmos,
creating a new world order.

Paragon of Virtue

There are licit shifts in the sky tonight
from dulcet blue to blackened shelter
lacing a canopy of empathy onto me.
The wonder of confession is held
fast in the heft of you, in the
strain that limits your smile.
So what if you are not all you
ought to be, your comforts are not
my business. My work is the forge,
the element, the piece of swarthy
soul. The perfect tangram fit.

Abstract

Your impossible voice strains to be heard
across endless inky nights, the darkness
ticking with envy.
Creatures stand buckled, waiting for your deep
impossible voice. Even I am craven, hollowed
out, cored, punctuated by longing.
Should you choose to speak, I will be first in line
to hear your impossible lies.

Possession

Searching for shells on a winter ruffled
beach, her eyes scan left to right reading
the close packed grains. Finding treasures
remains the quest every time.

A one-winged seabird appears in the surf
broken and listing, damage its strange new
veracity. She mirrors it, trying to see how that
would be.

Here, with Clare Island a slub on the horizon, a
gamut of birds alight whirling dervishes all. Here
is where she is not owned, borrowed, retrieved.
Not even rejected.

Here, on a day so clear the mountains are
blades cutting the eyes, the ocean draws and
swoops, gulping itself in. Here, now, and maybe
never again – she is the thief of her own life.

Lacunae

Tonight or some night soon
I will make a ledger of my life.
For death, you see, and to be
ready for the flighty kiss death
will place on me.
No doubt death will cast a
scathing glance at my accounting,
there seeing a lack of probity or
a vacuity of reason and excuse, such
as would change some sorry mangled
picture, elevate some minor omission
to the gold leaf of mistake.
The left side will show the incomings.
The right will peddle outgoings, strongly.
What I received and what I gave will elide
and smash off each other. Hulk boulders
roaring down a hill.
The unlikely stories, will not sit well with
pragmatic death. The bad decisions that
yielded good results will not balance, their
double effect snafu, shining bright.
Halfway through, I will address the notion
of fairness in things, the things one can't
control. The slicing arrows from left of field,
the uneven pitch.

I will add a note at base, so death can
see, that I am trying. Trying to show
that although I am the quick of my life, I
know I may not be the architect.

Asturias

for John Williams

You have to remember that the moment
of grace you had yesterday had sure
origin. Not sent by a haunting of spirits,
nor fluttering angels seeking a head to wreath.
No, nothing like that at all.
The moment of grace settled north of your
heart, under the clavicle, knitted in, steady
and strong, at the sound of a Spanish guitar
bestowing Asturias. Your soul turned in on
itself. Shy in the face of beauty.

Elba

Exile clings to him like a smell
of damp yarn, a low growl of
pain shoots into the atmosphere. A
missile obliterating the pretty stars.

No home now, no clay on his roots,
he searches feverishly for one sole scrap
of peace in this novel place that is not his own.
A bittersweet thought of the past life punctures
the organ of his skin, blistering whole areas in its
steady march to take up residence.

Self

Can we undo damage that
sits in the marrow burgeoning?
Bodies become sick turning
chaser on themselves, their cells
replicating, promiscuity their
very ethic. There are plans afoot
for you and they are not nebulous.
Can I tell you what you can do to?
thwart self ?
You can lay inky violets on a
lichened gravestone knowing there
are many layers between you and
them – the ancestors, or the ones not
concerned with your vacant howls.
Can I tell you what they might say to
you, if they even cared?
Look to the clay, lay down in it.
There it is, after all, where you will
coalesce. Always recognise the bad
as we all donate busily to build that
empty vessel. Assent to your
wounds like a salty flush heroine,
then paint your scar tissue with mercury.
Dull lazy silver – the opposite of the moon.

Early Afternoon

He drops with élan from the anglepoise lamp
eagerness his fuel, or so it seems.
Parachuting with bounce, the kind
of bounce lovers have in their arched step
en route to meet the beloved.

I let him crawl along the back of my hand to
exorcise skin memory of a brush with peril.
He visits for a while, then shimmies up his
silver cord. A cold hand closes around my throat.
Is he the visitor or am I?

Exposed

No one discerns the benefit of time,
the slow tick of a clock spooning in
on itself.
The illicit glancing touch of a lover's
fingers, burning the willing skin.
The benefit of time, all too soon, shows
how little we pin moments to the map
of our shameless hurry.

Shrug

Things break differently
with subtle rare
character, each to itself.
They break, things, they
do.
They crumble softly or
shatter bitterly. Things
break with ugsome haste
or sensate sloth.
Things break, I told you.
They do.

Tattoo

They say pain has no memory, no vigilant nous,
But here in the flimflam moment before the needle hits her
skin,
Before perception smacks reality, she wonders how they
Know this.
He appraises her fast, the youthful artist – sees her as a
fainter.
There is unspoken agreement, body to body, eye to eye,
The time frame is small.
The whip cracking, spine arching response to blunt pain sends
her
Flying through the corridors and old walls of her mind, to
conjure up
Any loved one's face – to stay the assault. But only a vandal
appears, a
Soul-snaring nomad.
Skin drawn taut between his fingers, the artist never looks up,
but
Tenses to her indrawn breath, shivery torso – his lips
compressing
Slightly and keeps going.
Finishing, cleaning up, end things, he looks at her and nods;
not a fainter
After all. This one knows more about her in twenty minutes,
than all the
Rest put together.

Aftermath

It was later, much later, that he saw
the capricious process that leads to
a smashing of two souls.
The thumbs of the gods bruised those
two berries, leaving a parallel stain of red
and black etched on the pale muslin of
their putative innocence.
To play with those liminal personae, the gods
set aside their other meddling, omniscient crouching.
There was too much chaotic delight to be had
in nomads and bards, and even the gods must
frolic sometimes.

Incongruity

I whispered to the healer of the
startling native vision I had one day.
He tried to believe my tale
and then proved he did not, speaking of
hallucinatory imaginings stalking my mind.
Probing my soft fontanels open once more,
the repetitious drumbeat of his scepticism
pummelled me down further, deeper into brain
manacles. Hating the insult that landed as a
drop of acid on my cheek, I swam upward, hard,
my brain built for war, a thrashing hunting shark
closing in from below on truth, to protest, to
lay my case. To no avail, to be flayed by qualm.

Beauty in Things Alone

After Johann C. Riedel

Eating glass, breaking it
down with mouth juice
the thinnest pieces are
hardest to manoeuvre, as
they migrate to cheek flesh
and marbled gum – the cutting
swift, deep, the between teeth
crackle pleases like no other, the
melting point – velvet.

Drowning in a City of Souls

At airports the unfurling
starts, the loosening to
be anyone or no one.
Watching others being
someone or one, though
there is always startle to
be had in the shadow ones.
Their hearts seem like the
viscera of seahorses, who
if you held them in your
palm would melt, their
clarity their very nemesis.

The Significant Child

On the express from Victoria, a baby boy in an
impossibly hi tech Hummer pram cries inconsolably,
his young parents taken aback by his militant
protestation.
Later I turn to check him, nudged by the
absence of ragged cries.
He lies in grandeur with a delicious pout, a world away.
I swoon at his beauty and pristine druid-like presence as he
trips across worlds I can only imagine.
This fast jostling carriage is nothing new to him,
A momentum.
In the womb he was hopped and hipped through the
every day, so he is home.

Penalty

Today the grass does not move
in a whipping tango or shiver like
desire in slender unison this way
or that, or even just one way showing
the endless bend that is love. Today
the juicy blades are stilled leaving time
to look up close, closer.
Like the hummingbird to the agave you
have long been drawn to the green. The
lush depth, the joyous. Just once, only
that once, you looked too long and
vanished.

Flashback

Climbing the stairs in a new house
You hear eerie creaks, settling groans.
Assaulted by irrational fear, you wonder
If they will hold for you, for others. What
If lightning strikes, or never does? Which
Would be worse?

But you know better. You felt it strike that
First day, short circuiting your spine. Laval
Heat pooling at base. You fold, and sit ash–
Still, remembering a face. The same face
That will slide over your death mask. And
Fit.

Trackers

Once, over many times she thinks about
fingerprints and the hints they leave on
the map of her being. That time he broke in
thrashing every corner of her bespoke bedroom,
scattering books and letters in a confetti deluge
of hate, pawing through lingerie and lace – the secret
things of the swift feminine.
Fastening his laser drug-hyped eyes on the bed
where she did not lie, whipping linen in turgid
fury. Later, good men came and it started all over
again. Dusting, speckling, lifting whorls – knowing
when they left, she would sweep up the imaginings
of letters, lace and dignity and burn them all.
The fingerprints on her skin are hints too, however brief
or incomplete, localised or imagined. These she could
lift
off with thin blade, preserve and graft onto a canvas in a
crazy totemic mosaic. Flakes of heady promise, flighty
as gold leaf. Small hints on the map of her being.

November

i.m. Tess

Tonight
I will blaspheme
the moon
as though it were
some sacred
thing and
then
challenge it
to a duel with
nervy sabre
because it shines
too bright
and I am not
ready to
be lone
again.

Lashed to the Bow

Any five in the morning is stirring
at Killadoon but this August fourth, fog
and sea mist vetch, costuming a distrait
shroud, banning island vistas,
calming oceanic pelt.

This then is what will break you, the beauty
or the kernel of pity within it. The chasmic
solitude or the stylish brutality of a no
that hunted a yes, or a mind so damned
to spit on reason, or a lash of queenly sea
spume hissing at the door.

Any five in the morning here, you might
whore your soul for the bond of the shore,
for the whim of the wave or the acumen of the
ocean; barter your human flesh, exorcise the rage
in the gore, for peace.

Seamed at the Hip

Damage heats our digits, laced
with gold. It seems the trusses of
pledge must settle with bands blasted
from deposits shorn.

Cyanogenic dawn leaching into soil, streams
Pooled, remainders of sulphurous greed.
All so we can flaunt fragile promise, on a
willing finger. To keep us safe.

Immer in das Leben verliebt*

She has wasted, this woman,
more emotion than necessary
on arid plains where nothing can
grow or step outside itself toward the
act of creation
Pushed the boat out into oceans
with no roil
Hoped for miracles in Amaranthine
gardens
Believed that good would rise above
not good, then was shown she did not
understand the provenance of
either
Sang in the mornings, never learning
there would be dusks deeper than any
night
Loved, though she kept no notes
or maps, so never saw it coming or
going
Learnt, in her amoebic stretch to
fit the world, that the world was
square, not round.

Always in love with life

Memento

The rose-tattooed china cup lies
in shards, robbed of its haughty
elegance by a blush terracotta
floor. Stifling a cry for a well loved
piece, I hunker down forensic hat
askew and imagine the glue that
would bring back my soft side; the
same clumsy fingers that felled it
would attune the restoration.
The flaws would be invisible to the
eye, but not to my eye. I gather it
up, an icy resolve creeping around the
nape of my neck, and cast it into the abyss.
You can never go back.

On Days of Nesting

Weight of minutes scares hours into
a howl and the swallows layer again
in a new house.
Knowing exactly where they are, you
tell no one, fearing the ignorance of retribution
and cleared gutters.
Sometimes you go to the attic furtively
to listen to their dulcet chatter and know that
they will be safe under your watch, your fierce avian
love.

Calliope Rises

Down deep down
south of my soul
you impressed me.
With your mesmeric
whispers I became
a puppet, a thing of no
will.
Had I not felt the refined
chill of your fingers, nor
the beat of your rowdy
pulse, I would deny you
three times.
Down deep down west of my soul
you impressed me.

Ways of Being

Holding tendrils of lemon balm in one hand,
snipped from the mother ship, I think of him.
Hopper and his Nighthawks.
Fathoming the connection over stunted minutes,
I bed the herb in, pressing, insisting.
Placing the pot on the floor inside my vitric cube,
I raise my arms, press against triple glass
and in one balletic move, pass through to the
other side.

Taharah

Your soul escapes out of lips worn
stretched in death.
They take the body you and others
lived in and now and then loved
wash tenderly through linen
covering inch by inch the warped
map that was your presence,
knowing it praises you,
this caring.

Forehead, silky eyelids
cheeks high, hollows beneath
Clavicle scooped, marbled defunct
breasts, ribs yet proud, hips jawed.
Onwards their hands push until
this body has been listened to. Would
that they had listened more in life,
would that you.

Gypsy

Not from nowhere
did this one come, with
the slow slide of the eyelid
over the grey orbit. Still as
ash and feral.

Not opposite not same but
the nudge of each. Upper lip
drawn taut skyward he scopes the
shoreline hard, making landfall
by moonlit night.

Gypsy Redux

The gypsy winters
here and there
alighting briefly to
pluck the splinters
from a thousand
human hearts.
Then returning once,
he subsumes a fierce
soul into his wintry
one. Though doubts
beset him, he casts them
aside braced by left right
logic, never once lifting
a mirror to his face. The sad
left eye, the barren sea.
All that is known of nature
lies on his sacred upper lip,
his visage a complete dominion,
his body a howling sculpt. His soul,
a room where strangers wander
marvelling at the caged fierce
one in museum fetters. A
testament to once.

Clouds

I swear I saw them as infants – why else would
I recognise them now? Why would I, writing, feel
like I am digging into peat bog, to excavate restless
cumuli? They almost suffocated me with their cottoness,
their charm, their Frankenstein taking – their hypoxic
tendrils drifting ever farther from me.
Why would I even care? Except this. Every single one is a word,
a shabby sigh ripped from my envious ribcage.

Per Se, Per Se

He made the incision under her
left breast, a rip and rend that she
dare not tack for fear of the
straight line
of perfect healing.

Anarchic artistry was his shovel as
he quarried the heart justly. Now
as she weeps, the dry eyes
gape on while the crazy breast
suppurates honestly.

Mask for Sale

Today Pierrot weeps for no one
his smooth face bereft of tears,
his hands at rest. A hanging
dove at either side of his body.
Being played as fool can only ingest so
many centuries, hurtling through time
trying to clasp the hem of her robe.
Bumbling & lovelorn, he arrived in
epoch twenty-one and upon awakening
found a shrink, took his Lexapro, and shook
his head at the wasted time.

Because I am vain

and know the sackcloth is not for me, nor the
tendency toward humility, promiscuous
in its swing for praise.
In my vanity, I need only nature and
the written word and the cool ice cloth
borne of reason, across my burning forehead.
To stay the rabble.

The Heart Uncut

It's strange how you sleep well now,
twice removed from land and self.
Strange how the prairie of your face
eludes me. Lately I wish you well, or
as well as mint beetles are liked by
many. With detached regard.
Stranger still, the way time holds you
and carries you alive through owlish
afternoons, your breath a lattice flung
upon a thousand vistas. Strange how a
fearful ego can remain intact, the
heart uncut. But listen, I want to know
if your spirit has healed? Have you
aligned peace with being, and have
I made myself clear? Finally.

The Length of Her Stretch

Unfurled from head to toe, suspended
between the tropics of Cancer and
Capricorn, her spine bounces on the
Equator.
Pushing hands and feet to the limit,
soaring over scorched lands, her
consciousness stirring to its outer rim,
scaring up strange empty parcels of
thought or non-thought, until her
toes dip in the freeze.
The snapback is consummate, ruthless,
visceral truth. Now she knows the
length of her stretch.

In the Beginning

In the room of ancient things
a small child bowls around,
a spinning top on calf legs.
Pointing at Botticelli's
effort, emitting volleys of
river flash words
No respecter she of the
reverent hush.
Renaissance and this moment
meld, and my four humours
sunder, melancholy pervading.
Having spent every drop of
passion in life, there will be none
left for the dying.

Actuarial Relief

Men ought not to marry
young, their readiness
physical means nothing
to the soul's desire,
fire is just fire.

Women need to be the
vessels for a while. They
marry in fecund haste but
there is time for second
acts, and third,
and waste.

Mystery Black

is my ink. Unscrewing the yacht bottle, in a quick flick
then opening you up, I insert the golden arrow into the sweep
bottle and the tongue nib seems to quiver in anticipation as
I twist and listen to you inhaling your life's blood with a sweet
hiss.
Nearly twenty five years of close piety rested in my left
hand, waiting as if in pain, while I grew thoughts out of
my head
like an ambush of once off, wayward cherry trees. Then
your whole
world is exposed to its *raison d'être*, as I make a stroke.
You have seen off other competitors, other loves, with
alacrity –
to tell your story.

Lefty, I too have paid a price awaiting your words. I
have grown
accustomed to you and your brush strokes, manic
bursts, and sulky
biting lips. It has been a dubious pleasure serving one of
the ten
per cent for so long, but listen dreamer poet, I know all about
your pragmatism. All lacquer on the outside then bayou
on the inside.
Just like me

Remember that time you packed me away for two years
or more
as if I was some detritus of your life. Two years in the
gloam. I refused
when you unpacked me. You had me sent off to some
hospital where
they restored my parts and I am new now. Not that you know.

There is one thing waiting, silently. I will say it out loud,
or as loud as your
wit will allow. My body is a forever piece of engineering,
yours is not.

Native Wave

Slough of stone slows
them down, sideways
descent working well.
Then hammered sand
set by tidal whim
emancipates the body and
they are warriors, shields
darned to the right. The
rhythm sets in and I hear
their steady battle prayer,
feel it in the blood, rising.
I see it in their innate
balletic run, onward toward the
wave, the cradle of the new
tribe, and what remains is the
primeval thrum.

The Bone Wife

There is a deftness she idly admires
in the way that he arranges the chains of
lacquered wishbones across the
window. A flick of the wrist settles
the melange into a delicate lattice
setting free the jewel colours. She
has painted each one to its contours
polishing the lacquer to a satiny
shine. Satisfied he turns to her and
they nod a complicit nod; there is
beauty in wishbones. Days later
when he is felled by a too frail and
bitter heart, she spends time with
each bone, tearing it apart. Calmly.

Mornings at Carrowniskey

A December morning wind
slaps your face harder than
any human hand, telling you
to go home, but the lure of
body and mind aligning with
the ocean is strong. Your empty
stomach leans into an icy spine
the same one that lacks courage
to face into the pain of love or loss,
to look closely at how much nerve
you have in the bank, or even, to
accept that you are shaken – because
in the end, you always wanted to live life
at full tilt. So, here now is the tilt – and what
are you going to do with it? The roaring
silver ocean owes you nothing though day
on day, you give it your soul love. The
hills and mountains to your right scoff at
your zany curdled mind and every step
embroiders the sting in deeper.
Your 'can't go on' moment is stilled by a thought
of him, *Vi faccio vedere come muore un Italiano,**
This is no foul comparison of courage in your mind,
much less will he go on, but, there is the memory of
ancestral fury forging through him – *You* cannot

remember his name but the ocean has not forgotten,
the earth has not forgotten, and you must not forget
how the elemental cosmos draws us in to itself each
day, making little of our thwarted humanity, bearing
gifts of clay, sea, and air.

*'Now you will see how an Italian dies.'
Fabrizio Quattrocchi – executed April 2004, Iraq.

There Are No Gods

Mornings watching the shore,
keeping vigil for the infinite,
staying the surprise invasion.
Below the pounding tide
a cottonfield blurs impossibly, sea salt
its fodder. You watch it all caring less about
anyone who is reckless enough to stay
here.
There is a reckoning too and it comes in
disguise, as if it were stalking you all along,
while you were busy scoping that same shore.
What you forgot was the fling back. The perfect sting.
The stranger making shore & not who you thought.
Not at all.

Lightning Source UK Ltd.
Milton Keynes UK
UKHW022015141020
371583UK00006B/353